# Ripley's Believe It or Not!

**Developed and produced by Ripley Publishing Ltd**

This edition published and distributed by:

Mason Crest
450 Parkway Drive, Suite D, Broomall, PA 19008
www.masoncrest.com

Printed and bound in the United States of America

First printing
9 8 7 6 5 4 3 2 1

Ripley's Believe It or Not!
Totally Bizarre
ISBN: 978-1-4222-3154-8 (hardback)
Ripley's Believe It or Not!—Complete 8 Title Series
ISBN: 978-1-4222-3147-0

Cataloging-in-Publication Data on file with the Library of Congress

PUBLISHER'S NOTE
While every effort has been made to verify the accuracy of the entries in this book, the
Publishers cannot be held responsible for any errors contained in the work. They would
be glad to receive any information from readers.

WARNING
Some of the stunts and activities in this book are undertaken by experts and should not
be attempted by anyone without adequate training and supervision.

# Ripley's Believe It or Not!

## Download The Weird

# TOTALLY
# BIZARRE

www.MasonCrest.com

# TOTALLY BIZARRE

**Incredibly Strange. Step inside
the world of the unexpected. Check out
the eye-popping brothers, the bike
made from lobsters, and the phone
booth filled with fish!**

Joshua Carter can touch his shoulders
together in front of his chest, because he
was born without collarbones...

One of the world's bloodiest sports has to be fluorescent-light fighting, during which Japanese professional wrestlers batter each other into submission with long glass rods. After just a few minutes, both fighters are left covered in blood, and broken glass is strewn around the ring. There is a referee, but the general rules of the contest seem to be that anything goes. Extreme sports fans love the extra violence and bloodshed so much that it has spawned a whole new range of gimmicky contests in Japanese wrestling, using weapons such as barbed wire, weed whackers, TV sets, folding chairs, cheese graters, and cacti!

## BALLOON MAN

In a million-to-one freak accident, New Zealand truck driver Steven McCormack's body was inflated to three times its original size when a compressed air nozzle pierced his left buttock.

The 48-year-old was working on his truck at Opotiki on the North Island in May 2011 when he slipped between the cab and the trailer, dislodging the compressed air hose that feeds the brakes. The nozzle pierced his left buttock, sending air compressed to 100 lb (45 kg) per square inch rushing into his body. As his neck, feet, and hands swelled up instantly, he began to scream for fear that he was about to explode. "I had no choice but to just lay there, blowing up like a balloon," he said. Workmates hurried to his aid, and he was rushed to the hospital where his lungs were drained and a surgical drill was used to clear the wound in his buttock, leaving a hole about 1 in (2.5 cm) wide and 2 in (5 cm) deep. Doctors later told him they were surprised the compressed air did not make his skin burst.

**PLASTIC BIRDS** Keen bird-watchers Ken and Fay Jackson spent an entire day observing two owls on the roof of an apartment block opposite their home in Torquay, England— before realizing that the birds were made of plastic. The couple thought the reason the owls had not moved at all during that time was because they were stalking prey.

**FASHION VICTIM** Accused of shoplifting from a local store, Stephen Kirkbride turned up in court in Kendal, Cumbria, England, wearing the exact coat he denied stealing.

**PEAK CONDITION** A 4x4 vehicle was abandoned near the top of the 3,560-ft-high (1,085-m) Mount Snowdon in Wales twice in a month in 2011. On the second occasion— September 29—it had a "For Sale" sign attached to the windshield.

**IMPROPER ADDRESS** Australian Thomas John Collins was jailed in November 2010 for calling Magistrate Matthew McLaughlin "mate" twice during a hearing in Ipswich, Queensland.

**WRONG WARRANT** Police searched the home of Rose and Walter Martin of Brooklyn, New York, more than 50 times in eight years owing to a computer error.

**TALKING GARBAGE** As part of the war on litter, British councils introduced garbage bins that say "thank you," applaud, or even burp when trash is dropped into them. In Sweden, a talking bin received three times more trash than a regular one nearby.

**WRONG SIDE** A senior citizen from Jena, Germany, who wanted to block off the entrance to his cellar, worked from the wrong side of the new partition and ended up accidentally bricking himself into the cellar for several days.

**LUCKY LANDING** Five-year-old Ye Zixu escaped with just scratches and bruises after falling from the window of a tenth-floor apartment in Chongqing, China. Luckily, her 100-ft (30-m) fall was broken when she landed on a ground-floor awning.

**LAUGHING FITS** Pseudobulbar affect (PBA) is a neurological condition in which patients are unable to control sudden outbursts of crying or laughter. Episodes can last for several minutes, and a patient might laugh uncontrollably even when angry or frustrated.

**LONGEST EARRING** U.S.-based Romanian jewelry designer Adrian Haiduc spent eight months creating an earring that is almost a third of a mile (0.5 km) long. The world's longest earring measures 1,550 ft (472 m) in length and is made from crystals, pearls, gemstones, and beads, all strung on silk. It features three strings—one worn in the hair, another forming a necklace, and the third hanging as a conventional earring.

**FUNERAL CLOWN** John Brady of Drimnagh, Ireland, runs a funeral clown company, Dead Happy Ireland, for people looking to put the "fun" into "funeral." The company ad reads: "We bring squirting flowers, we make balloon animals. We can even fall into the grave if you want us to. Let your loved one go down with a smile."

**MUMMIFIED PASSENGER** Unsure what to do when her homeless friend died in her car, a Californian woman drove the partially mummified corpse around for ten months. On investigating the car, police officers were confronted with a foul stench and a leg poking out from under a blanket.

## FLUSHED FRENCHMAN

A high-speed TGV train traveling between La Rochelle and Paris was delayed for two hours after a 26-year-old passenger dropped his mobile phone into the onboard toilet. He attempted to retrieve the device, but his arm became jammed in the toilet system and would not budge. The driver stopped the train, but even French firefighters could not extricate the man's arm from the toilet bowl. In order for the train to continue its journey, the firefighters were forced to remove the entire toilet from the carriage, with the man still attached.

**When did you first discover you could pop your eyes out?**
**Antonio:** I was seven years old and it was an accident. I was combing through my big Afro hair and the comb got stuck. As I pulled it out, my left eye popped out of its socket at the same time! After it happened this first time, I found I could control it myself and showed my mum, who took me straight to the hospital where they asked me if I could pop the right eye out, too, and I could.
**Hugh:** I discovered I could do it only just over a year ago now, but didn't tell anyone straightaway—it's a fairly new thing for me.

**Does it hurt when you do it? Antonio:** No, not at all. Once when I pushed them out too far they hurt a little, but that was a one-off. My eyes do get tired when I am popping them on a daily basis, but I can see perfectly, so I know it isn't affecting my health.
**Hugh:** It feels uncomfortable because I don't do it all the time like Antonio and it can sometimes make my vision blurry, but Antonio's doctor has said that it is not harmful to my sight, so I am

not worried about any long-term effects at this stage.

**How has eye-popping changed your life?**
**Antonio:** Since being on Britain's Got Talent, I get stopped in the street and asked to pop my eyes about 200 to 300 times a day.
**Hugh:** When I am walking down the street with Antonio, he often is stopped and asked to pop his eyes out for a picture. They always ask me if I can pop mine out, too, and I say no, but when they take the picture I pop mine, too! Always gets a few laughs, so that is nice.

**Can you explain to us how you do it? Antonio:** Not really! All I know is there are three muscles at the back of your eye and you can compress them, and if you do this and push the eye forward at the same time you get the desired popping result.
**Hugh:** It's tricky! The only way I can explain it, is it is like opening your eye as wide as you can, by pushing your top and bottom eyelids back, and then pushing the muscles at the back of your eye as hard as you can until the eye pops out. But I wouldn't try it at home like us!

# Eye Poppers

Brothers Hugh (left) and Antonio Francis from Essex, England, can pop their eyes out of their sockets. Antonio, who has been able to do this since childhood, has demonstrated his eye-boggling skill on *Britain's Got Talent* and in a music video for electropop act Hot Chip.

# BAT SOUP

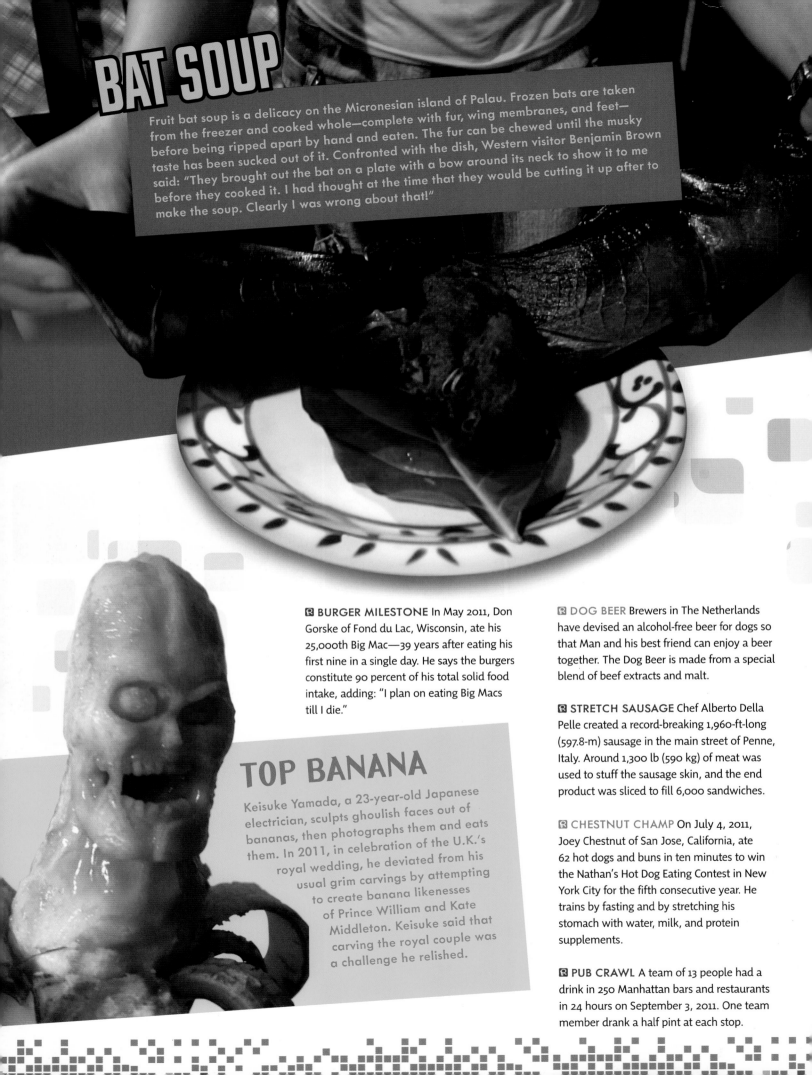

Fruit bat soup is a delicacy on the Micronesian island of Palau. Frozen bats are taken from the freezer and cooked whole—complete with fur, wing membranes, and feet—before being ripped apart by hand and eaten. The fur can be chewed until the musky taste has been sucked out of it. Confronted with the dish, Western visitor Benjamin Brown said: "They brought out the bat on a plate with a bow around its neck to show it to me before they cooked it. I had thought at the time that they would be cutting it up after to make the soup. Clearly I was wrong about that!"

**BURGER MILESTONE** In May 2011, Don Gorske of Fond du Lac, Wisconsin, ate his 25,000th Big Mac—39 years after eating his first nine in a single day. He says the burgers constitute 90 percent of his total solid food intake, adding: "I plan on eating Big Macs till I die."

## TOP BANANA

Keisuke Yamada, a 23-year-old Japanese electrician, sculpts ghoulish faces out of bananas, then photographs them and eats them. In 2011, in celebration of the U.K.'s royal wedding, he deviated from his usual grim carvings by attempting to create banana likenesses of Prince William and Kate Middleton. Keisuke said that carving the royal couple was a challenge he relished.

**DOG BEER** Brewers in The Netherlands have devised an alcohol-free beer for dogs so that Man and his best friend can enjoy a beer together. The Dog Beer is made from a special blend of beef extracts and malt.

**STRETCH SAUSAGE** Chef Alberto Della Pelle created a record-breaking 1,960-ft-long (597.8-m) sausage in the main street of Penne, Italy. Around 1,300 lb (590 kg) of meat was used to stuff the sausage skin, and the end product was sliced to fill 6,000 sandwiches.

**CHESTNUT CHAMP** On July 4, 2011, Joey Chestnut of San Jose, California, ate 62 hot dogs and buns in ten minutes to win the Nathan's Hot Dog Eating Contest in New York City for the fifth consecutive year. He trains by fasting and by stretching his stomach with water, milk, and protein supplements.

**PUB CRAWL** A team of 13 people had a drink in 250 Manhattan bars and restaurants in 24 hours on September 3, 2011. One team member drank a half pint at each stop.

® **LARGE GLASS** An enormous wine glass measuring 7 ft 10 in (2.4 m) high and 5 ft 5 in (1.6 m) in diameter was unveiled at a wine festival in Beirut, Lebanon, in October 2010. The giant goblet-shaped container was created by engineers Walid Richa and Moussa Zakharia from Plexiglas, and was only one-quarter full after having 100 bottles of wine emptied into it.

® **SARDINE CURE** Patients in Hyderabad, India, eat live sardines coated in masala, a spice mix, to cure their asthma. The treatment is administered by 200 members of the Goud family one day in June each year, and several hundred thousand people with respiratory problems line up to eat the 2-in-long (5-cm) spicy fish, the recipe for which is said to have been handed down by a Hindu saint.

® **ROBOT WAITERS** Samurai robot waiters serve customers at the Hajime Restaurant in Bangkok, Thailand. Every 30 minutes the robot waiters stop what they are doing and break into a dance.

® **RELIABLE REFRIGERATOR** A General Electric refrigerator bought in 1952 has enjoyed some 60 years of continuous use in the Oxford, England, home of Doris Stogdale. The fridge—bought for the equivalent of $200 in today's money—has never needed any maintenance or even a single new part.

® **COLOSSAL CORGI** As part of the buildup to the 2011 royal wedding between Prince William and Kate Middleton, British cake designer Michelle Wibowo created a giant cake in the shape of a royal corgi dog. The cake measured nearly 6 x 4 ft (1.8 x 1.2 m) and weighed 150 lb (68 kg).

® **RARE WINE** At a sale in Geneva, Switzerland, in November 2010, a rare large Imperial bottle of 1947 French Cheval-Blanc white wine—equal to eight standard bottles—was sold to a private collector for $304,375. Labeled "the greatest wine ever made," it is so coveted that enthusiasts have traveled thousands of miles to taste it.

® **WINNING SEQUENCE** After getting engaged on 10/10/10 and registering a court marriage on 11/11/11, Brandon Pereira and Emilia D'Silva maintained the sequence by having a traditional church wedding in Mumbai, India, at noon on 12/12/12.

® **TIMELY WARNING** J.D. Mullane, of Middletown, New Jersey, has a grandfather clock that never runs but has chimed on several occasions—and every time a child was in danger. It also chimes every April, the month of the death of his sister, Mary Beth, from whom he inherited the clock in 2002.

*Recipe (for those with strong stomachs): serves 4*

### Ingredients
3 well-washed fruit bats, skinned and gutted if you prefer
1 tablespoon finely sliced fresh ginger
1 large onion, quartered
Soy sauce and/or coconut cream
Chopped scallions
Sea salt to taste

### Method
Place bats in a large kettle and cover with water. Add ginger, onion, and salt. Bring to a boil, then lower the heat and simmer for 45 minutes. Strain the broth into a second kettle. Remove the bat meat from the bones if you prefer, then return it with any desired innards to the broth. Sprinkle with scallions and season with soy sauce and/or coconut cream.

# Light Fantastic

Rashad Alakbarov, an artist from Azerbaijan, installed this unique artwork in the Phillips de Pury gallery in London, England, in 2012. The "painting" is actually white light projected through 90 plexiglass model airplanes suspended from the ceiling. The image depicts Baku, the capital of Azerbaijan on the Caspian Sea.

**HEADSHOT HERO** Sergeant Paul "Headshot" Boothroyd earned his nickname after surviving a sniper's bullet to the head while serving in Helmand Province, Afghanistan, in March 2011. Just 15 minutes after being shot, he was smoking a cigarette and walking unaided to a military helicopter. Doctors say the survival rate for being shot in the head is only about one in 10,000.

Over a period of two years, James Ford, an art student in Nottingham, England, collected his own boogers on a daily basis and molded them into a ¾-in-diameter (21-mm) ball—about the size of a Brussels sprout. He collected the boogers in an eggcup and then glued them together to create his mucus mosaic, which has been exhibited in London and Lithuania.

**HOTEL FALL** Four-year-old Jo Williams fell seven stories from a hotel balcony in Miami, Florida, but landed without breaking a sin bone. He hit several palm trees on the way down.

**ATOMIC KITCHEN** A man was arrested in 2011 after attempting to split atoms in the kitchen of his home in southern Sweden. He said it was simply a hobby, but after creating a small meltdow on his stove, he was arrested for unauthori possession of nuclear material—radium, americium, and uranium.

**MEDICAL MESSAGE** To ensure that she does not endure a lingering death, 81-year-old grandmother Joy Tomkins from Norfolk, England, has tattooed the words "Do Not Resuscitate" across her chest. In case she collapses face down and paramedics miss the big blue letters, she has also had "P.T.O." and an arrow inked on her back.

**"MALE" MOM** Jackie Kelly of Blountsto Florida, was incorrectly listed as a male on birth certificate and has officially been a m since 1958—even though she has two child

**MOHICAN GATHERING** 109 staff and students gathered in a room at West Cheshire College, England, on September 16, 2011—all sporting Mohican haircuts.

**CUTTING EDGE** A $100,000 shaving razor has gone on sale featuring white sapp blades that last forever and have an edge less than 100 atoms wide—5,000 times thinner than the width of a hair. Designed b a Portland, Oregon, company, the razor ha a handle made mainly from iridium, a met derived almost entirely from meteorites an ten times rarer than platinum.

**WEIGHT ISSUES** Believed to be one of the fattest kids in the world, Suman Khatun from West Bengal, India, weighed a staggering 201 lb (91 kg) when she was just six years old and 3 ft 5 in (1.03 m) tall—more than five times her recommended weight, and the same weight as a Great Dane. In an average week, she ate 31 lb (14 kg) of rice, 18 lb (8 kg) of potatoes, 18 lb (8 kg) of fish, and about 180 bananas, as well as assorted cream cakes and her favorite Bengali sweets.

**COMBAT GNOMES** Shawn Thorsson o Petaluma, California, has created a range o Combat Garden Gnomes—regular gnomes wielding army rifles—which he sells online The U.S. Naval Reserve officer claims he ca up with the idea because he wanted a mili presence in his garden.

OLICE VULTURES Police chiefs in Germany
d three vultures—named Sherlock,
mbo, and Miss Marple—to replace sniffer
s in the hope that the birds' amazing
ight, sense of smell, and ability to locate
d prey would help them to find missing
es. However, the scheme was abandoned
the disinterested vultures managed only to
a cadaver when it was placed immediately
ont of their beaks.

ENTIL SPROUT A 4,000-year-old lentil seed
d during a 2008 archeological excavation in
hya Province, Turkey, germinated and
uted the following year.

## FISH PHONE

Japan, was filled with hundreds
11. The unusual aquarium was a
signed to raise awareness of the
production of such fish in Japan.

R BORDER CROSSINGS Baarle-Hertog,
Belgium, and Baarle-Nassau, the Netherlands,
make up a single town with twisted borders.
Walking only a few streets, it is possible to
cross national borders half a dozen times!

R COMPLEX CHOCOLATE U.S. scientists
have discovered that humans are less
genetically complex than chocolate biscuits.
Humans have 20–25,000 genes, but cacao,
from which we make chocolate, has 35,000.

R ODD PASSENGER A 59-year-old woman
was arrested in Chesterton, Indiana, after being
caught driving a golf cart while drunk and in
the company of a large scarecrow.

R EXPLODING TOILETS Two workers at a
federal building in Washington, D.C., suffered
cuts after a plumbing malfunction caused
two toilets to explode and send tiny shards
of porcelain flying through the air. The 2,500
employees in the building were warned not to
use the bathrooms until the problem was fixed.

# Seal Surprise

An adventurous fur seal pup gave the occupant of a house in Tauranga, New Zealand, a shock when it visited in December 2011. The seal had made its way from the nearby harbor, across a busy road and slipped through a cat flap, before making itself comfortable on the couch for the night, apparently not bothered by the resident cats and dogs. As seals can give a nasty bite, a wildlife official was deployed to recover the animal, and "Lucky," as the seal was named after his traffic-dodging abilities, was released back into the sea.

🅡 **IN CUFFS** A criminal suspect escaped from a police station in Buffalo, New York State, on April 26, 2011... while still wearing handcuffs. When police rearrested him, they added a new charge for stealing the handcuffs in his possession.

🔺 **THE GRIZZLY BEAR CAN RUN AS FAST AS THE AVERAGE HORSE.** ◢

🅡 **MEMORY MAN** Aurelien Hayman of Cardiff, Wales, can remember what he had to eat, what he did, what was in the news, and even what the weather was like on any given day dating back over a decade. He is one of very few people with hyperthymesia, or highly superior autobiographical memory.

🅡 **FOX'S REVENGE** A hunter in Belarus was shot in the leg by a fox in January 2011. As the man attempted to club the fox to death with his rifle after shooting it, the animal's paw struck the trigger, firing the gun.

🅡 **SMELLY SIREN** A Japanese smoke alarm for deaf people emits such a powerful smell that those asleep wake up within 2½ minutes of the stench hitting them. Instead of a shrill wail, the device releases the chemical compound allyl isothiocyanate, which is what gives horseradish, mustard, and wasabi their bite.

🅡 **TWO FUNERALS** Romania's fattest man, 870-lb (395-kg) Cristian Capatanescu, had postmortem liposuction so that half of him could be buried in a regular-sized coffin and the other half cremated. His family asked doctors to remove some of his bulk because they couldn't afford an extra-large reinforced coffin.

🅡 **PIPE HOME** Mao Li, 30, lived for a year in a 6-ft-long (1.8-m) concrete flood pipe beside a bridge in Haikou, China. Squeezing feet first into the narrow opening, he installed a wood floor, a door, rugs, and cushions.

# SNAKE INVADER

A giant Burmese Python captured in the Florida Everglades in October 2011 was one of the largest ever found in the state. When biologists performed an autopsy on the 15¾-ft-long (4.8-m) reptile, they discovered a recently swallowed 76-lb (34-kg) adult deer, still remarkably intact. It was the largest prey ever found inside a Florida snake. As their name suggests, Burmese Pythons are not native to Florida—the wild population, now in the tens of thousands, is thought to have grown from pet snakes that escaped in the 1990s.

Over 1,000 people—including superheroes—have re-created childhood pictures for an Internet project titled "Young Me/Now Me." It is the brainchild of Los Angeles-based web personality Ze Frank, who asks visitors to his site to submit a photo of their younger self along with another one as they are today in roughly the same pose, hence the lack of smiles on the faces of these superhero brothers!

# YOUNG ME, NOW ME

**ICE RIDE** Michal Kawolski of Gdansk, Poland, had to be rescued by coastguards after drifting half a mile out to sea on a sheet of ice. He had been testing the strength of the ice next to the shore, when a piece suddenly broke away and strong currents carried him out into the Baltic Sea.

**HEAT HYPNOSIS** In December 2010, staff at a small shoe repair shop in Bromsgrove, England, were shivering in temperatures of 8°F (−13°C) until their boss had them hypnotized into thinking they were warm. Martin Connellan always kept the door to the shop open and had tried buying jackets for his workers, but when that failed he brought in hypnotist Jim Kerwin— and after just five minutes under hypnosis some staff were complaining about how hot they were.

**BURIED FINGERS** Playing near Paris, France, a seven-year-old schoolboy dug up a glass jar containing several well-preserved human fingers thought to belong to a local carpenter who lost four digits in an accident more than 30 years before. At the time the carpenter's fingers could not be surgically reattached, so he put them in a jar full of alcohol and buried them near his home.

**BAD DRIVER** Gageen Preet Singh of Surrey, England, was paid up to £800 a time by driving test candidates to take the test on their behalf—yet he himself was such a bad driver that he repeatedly failed the tests. Out of eight tests he was known to have taken for clients, he failed five. To carry out the illegal impersonations, he used an array of disguises, including fake mustaches and wigs.

# TINY BIKE

This tiny electric bike, called Mooshiqk (which means mouse in Sanskrit), measures only 13 inches in height and weighs just 11 lbs (5 kg). It can be ridden by an adult man and can travel at speeds of up to 12 mph (20 km/h).

**PASTA HAT** Austrian atheist Niko Alm has won the right to be shown on his driver's license photo wearing a pasta strainer as "religious headgear." Mr. Alm, who belongs to the Church of the Flying Spaghetti Monster, said the sieve was a requirement of his religion, pastafarianism.

# Lobster Bike

Taiwanese chef and food-carving expert Huang Mingbo shows off his artistic culinary creation "Lobster Motorcycle," made from five lobster shells, in Fujian Province, China.

# Smallest Man

A 72-year-old Nepalese man, unknown outside his remote village until 2012, has been recognized as the world's smallest man. Chandra Bahadur Dangi stands just 21.5 in (54.6 cm) tall and weighs only 32 lb (14.5 kg). He is 5 in (13 cm) shorter than his compatriot and previous record holder, Khagendra Thapa Magar.

**MYSTERY DEATH** An Irish coroner ruled that a man who burned to death in his home on December 22, 2010, died of spontaneous human combustion. The totally burned body of Michael Faherty, 76, was found lying face down near an open fire in his living room in Galway, but coroner Dr. Ciaran McLoughlin ruled that the fire was not the cause of the fatal blaze. The only damage was to the body, the ceiling immediately above, and the floor directly beneath.

**PERFECT SYMMETRY** Richard Burton Vail of Ontario, Canada, had birth and death dates that mirrored each other as a palindrome—11-12-20 and 02-21-11.

**STORED BODIES** Jean Stevens of Wyalusing, Pennsylvania, kept her deceased husband's body in her home for a decade—and her twin sister's body for a year. When the authorities found out, they agreed she could keep them if she built a separate building to store them in.

**BAD CHOICE** Stopped by traffic police in Great Falls, Montana, a man who had three outstanding warrants for his arrest gave officers a false name—but finished up in custody anyway because the name he gave was also that of a wanted man!

**GUMMY HEART** Los Angeles candy man David Klein invented an unusual new line for Valentine's Day 2011—a 2-lb-8-oz (1.1-kg), throbbing, anatomically correct gummy heart that oozed candy blood in 11 places. He also marketed an edible bleeding nose and a gummy severed foot with a gangrenous toe.

**100-MPH COUCH** A two-seater brown leather couch, fitted with a motorcycle engine, clocked a top speed of 101 mph (163 km/h) at Camden Airport near Sydney, Australia, in September 2011, making it the world's fastest sofa. Designed by Paul McKinnon and driven by Glenn Suter, the superfast sofa came complete with a coffee table to help the contraption's aerodynamics.

**COFFIN BED** Every Friday night since 1988, Zeli Rossi of Minas Gerais, Brazil, has traded his bed for a coffin. Rossi and a friend struck a deal many years ago that whoever died first would have his coffin bought by the other. Rossi's friend bought him a coffin when he mistakenly thought Rossi had died in a 1983 car crash, so when the friend died five years later, Rossi started sleeping in the coffin to honor his memory.

**BACK FROM THE DEAD** A morgue in Malatya Province, Turkey, has been built with a special motion-detecting alarm system—in case "dead" bodies come back to life. If a patient, declared dead by doctors, suddenly wakes up, the movement sets off an alarm in the mortuary's refrigerators, which also have doors that can be opened from the inside.

**WASHROOM STOLEN** In March 2011, thieves stole a 198-lb (90-kg) gray-and-white portable washroom from ski trails near Bognor, Canada.

**R** PARTING SHOT Alabama company Holy Smoke offers to ensure that deceased gun-lovers go out with a bang by turning their ashes into ammunition that can be fired by relatives.

**R** TAX BILL In 2011, Martine Courtois of Bruyeres, France, received a $16 land inheritance tax bill in the name of her grandfather, Pierre Barotte, who died in 1949.

**R** WIFE DUPED To be rid of his wife, a U.K. immigration officer secretly added her name to a list of suspected terrorists while she was in Pakistan visiting her family, meaning that she was unable to fly back to Britain for three years until his deception was uncovered. The truth came out only when he applied for promotion at work and was asked about his wife being a terrorist. He confessed to the deception and was fired for gross misconduct.

**R** SHELF LIFE Charles Jones Jr. lived unnoticed in the basement of the Ocean Township Library, New Jersey, for nearly two weeks in 2010.

**R** LOCKED IN BATHROOM A 69-year-old woman from Paris, France, survived being locked in the bathroom of her second-floor apartment for three weeks after the door lock broke off in her hand. She tried to summon help by banging on the wall with her shoe night and day, but neighbors ignored the noise.

**R** CAR PLUNGE Austrian teenagers Jürgen Oster and Felix Lemann escaped serious injury when their car plunged over the side of a Swiss mountain pass and crashed 900 ft (274 m) to the valley floor with such force that the vehicle folded in half.

**R** MOON SUIT U.S. patent 3,139,622 was issued in 1964 for an astronaut moon suit. It had a large dish on the helmet to reflect solar radiation away from the astronaut.

**R** T PARTY Students at Georgia Tech in Atlanta have been removing the letter "T" from signs all over the campus, a prank that has cost the school over $100,000 in repairs. The tradition of stealing the "T" off Tech Tower began in the 1960s, but has spread to stadium signs and even book bins in front of the library.

**R** DIED TWICE In January 2011, Pinnitla Varalakshmi of Andhra Pradesh, India, was declared dead twice in 24 hours. She awoke as she was being prepared for her funeral, but then died for real shortly afterward.

# DOLPHIN TATTOO

Heine Braeck, from Sarpsborg in Norway, lost his right arm in an accident on a railway line when he was a teenager, 20 years ago. Now, he has decided to make an unusual feature of his amputation by enlisting the help of tattoo artist Valio Ska to paint over his shortened upper arm so that it looks like a dolphin. Heine had always thought his arm looked like a dolphin's head, which is why he chose this animal for his tattoo.

# WORM DELICACY

People in the Philippines eat a saltwater bivalve mollusk that bores into wooden ships, piers, and docks. Known as a shipworm, because of its wormlike appearance and taste for wood, it can also be taken with rum as an aphrodisiac—a concoction called tamilok. Filipino Lloyd Lumbania says: "Tamilok is best eaten raw with a dash of lime juice. It tastes like raw oyster, is a bit salty and slimy, and smells like rotten wood."

# ACQUIRED TASTES

- **MONKEY BRAINS**
  These are eaten, often raw, in some Asian countries.

- **RAW SQUID**
  For the Japanese dish of *ika sashimi*, the thinly sliced raw squid is usually so fresh it's still moving when you eat it.

- **STEAMED RATS**
  These are on the menu at a wild game restaurant in southern China.

- **TARANTULA SPIDERS**
  Deep fried in salt and garlic, these are widely consumed throughout Cambodia.

- **SNAKE WINE**
  In Vietnam, you can drink wine with a dead snake still in the bottle.

- **FRIED CATTLE TESTICLES**
  In the American Midwest and central Canada, Rocky Mountain Oysters—otherwise known as fried cattle testicles—are consumed.

- **FROG FALLOPIAN TUBES**
  *Hasma*, a popular Chinese dessert, consists of the dried fallopian tubes of frogs.

- **COOKED GOAT BRAINS**
  The Mexican dish *cabeza de cabrito* involves eating the cooked brains of a goat directly out of the animal's brain cavities.

- **ASIAN BAT PASTE**
  This is prepared by boiling a live bat in milk and then mashing it into a pulp.

- **JELLIED MOOSE NOSE**
  In parts of Canada, you can eat jellied moose nose, where the severed nose is boiled into a jelly before being served chilled.

🅡 **KEEN GARDENER** Thomas Jefferson (1743–1826), the third U.S. president, grew 170 different fruits and 330 types of herbs and vegetables at his Monticello, Virginia, home.

🅡 **BUTTER SCULPTURES** As a tribute to the space shuttle program's 30-year legacy, the 2011 Ohio State Fair displayed butter sculptures of the shuttle and an astronaut, alongside its traditional butter sculptures of a cow and a calf. The exhibit took 475 hours to create and used 1,550 lb (703 kg) of butter —about 6,200 sticks.

🅡 **DOG LOVERS** In the course of "Hot Dog Season," from Memorial Day to Labor Day, Americans consume an average of 7 billion hot dogs, which works out at 818 hot dogs being eaten every second.

🅡 **DEVIL'S TOOL** In the Middle Ages, the fork was seen as the tool of the Devil. It did not become a popular dining implement until the 17th century, when the French nobility needed something for eating their new favorite food: peas.

🅡 **VERY SMELLY FISH** Some airlines and Swedish apartment complexes have banned *surströmming*, a delicacy of fermented herring, owing to its intense, rotten odor that makes it one of the world's worst-smelling foods.

🅡 **LETTUCE LOVER** Elsie Campbell of Derby, England, used to eat four whole lettuces a day. She would eat a whole lettuce at work, and then go home and eat more and more, cutting them into chunks like a watermelon.

🅡 **TOP POPSICLE** The Marquis Los Cabos resort in Baja California Sur, Mexico, has launched a popsicle selling for $1,000. Although served on an ordinary plastic stick the popsicle is made from premium tequila, which sells for $1,500 a bottle, and also contains 24-carat gold flakes.

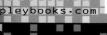

# Cabbage Head

Russian artist Dimitri Tsykalov uses an ax, a saw, and an electric drill to carve scary human skulls out of fresh fruit and vegetables, including melons, apples, and cabbages. With surgical precision, he then uses a scalpel, pincers, and cotton-wool pads to add authentic detail. Finally, he waits for his sculptures to rot before photographing them. "The flies let me know when it's time to take a picture," he says.

# The Greatest

The 1903 lineup at Barnum & Bailey's Circus included a classic Bearded Lady, several "Lilliputians," and many other novelty acts. Founded by showmen P.T. Barnum and James Anthony Bailey in 1881, and billing itself as "The Greatest Show on Earth," the circus enjoyed tremendous success in the United States and Europe, exhibiting bizarre and unusual performers alongside animal acts such as Jumbo the world's largest elephant, performing geese, and musical donkeys.

# Show on Earth

1 Mohammed Soliman, Whirling Dervish and Fire-eater  2 Ivy Howard, Contortionist  3 John Hayes, Tattooed Man  4 Leah May, Giantess (8 ft 3½ in/2.53 m)
5 Young Herrman, Expansionist (expands chest measurement by 13¾ in/35 cm)  6 Maxey, Needle Eater  7 George Tomasso, Human Pincushion
8 John/James William Coffey, Skeleton Man  9 Edith Clifford, Sword Swallower  10 James Morris, Elastic Skin Man  11 William Doss, Telescope Neck Man
12 Annie Howard  13 Vera Wren, Female Boxer  14 Billy Wells, Hard-headed Man  15 Hovart family of Lilliputians  16 Beautiful Marie, Human Mountain
17 Hovart family of Lilliputians  18 Krao Farini, Missing Link  19 Hovart family of Lilliputians  20 Lionel the Lion-faced Boy  21 Hovart family of Lilliputians
22 Grace Gilbert, Bearded Lady  23 Charles Tripp, Armless Wonder  24 Hovart family of Lilliputians  25 Albino "Rob Roy," Wild Man of Scotland

*Last Veil*

For her wedding to Ferdinand Pucci near Naples, Italy, bride Elena De Angelis wore the world's longest wedding veil, measuring an unbelievable 1.8 mi (3 km) long. The white silk veil, which was 6 ft 6 in (2 m) wide, took months to make and needed a staggering 600 people to carry it. The village of Casal di Principe came to a standstill as hundreds of people turned out to help her along the streets to the church. Her veil was so long, it would take Usain Bolt racing at world-record top speed nearly 5 minutes to run its length.

Joshua Carter from Leesburg, Georgia, can touch his shoulders together in front of his chest, but don't try this yourself. Joshua was born without collarbones, which means that he has hypermobile, or double-jointed, shoulders. The collarbone normally forms a strut between the shoulder blade and the breastbone, and is the only long bone in the body that lies horizontal. "Having no collarbones is advantage," says Joshu "it has allowed me to f into small spaces and w through a crowd easily!

⚡ **HARD LABOR** In August 2011, an 11-year-old boy in Aachen, Germany, called police to complain that his mother kept making him do chores around the house during the school summer holidays.

⚡ **FAMILY TRADITION** Four generations of one family have got married on September 9—a tradition stretching back more than a century. Angelynn Perchermeier was wed in Cincinnati, Ohio, on September 9, 2011 —100 years to the day that her great-great-grandparents had exchanged their vows. Her great-grandparents and her grandparents also chose September 9 for their weddings.

⚡ **BUSY LIFE** Ancentus Akuku of Kisumu, Kenya, married more than 100 times and sired more than 160 children before his death on October 3, 2010, aged 94.

⚡ **TIGHT SPOT** Prisoner Juan Ramirez Tijerina tried to escape from a jail in Chetumal, Mexico, by packing himself into his girlfriend's suitcase. When suspicious guards opened her bag, they found Ramirez curled up in the fetal position wearing only his underpants and socks.

⚡ **LEGO TOWER** Over a period of four days in April 2011, 6,000 LEGO® lovers joined forces to build a LEGO tower standing more than 102 ft (31 m) high in São Paulo, Brazil. The tower, which was composed of 500,000 LEGO bricks, was stacked up with the help of a crane and was held in place by wire supports to stop it toppling over in the wind.

⚡ **SEWER ORDEAL** In October 2010, Daniel Collins of Raymore, Missouri, fell into a sewer and was swept through more than a mile (1.6 km) of pipe before he was rescued. He was working in the sewage system when his safety line unhooked and the water pushed him along the 2-ft-wide (0.6-m) pipe, finally dumping him in a 12-ft-deep (3.6-m) chamber.

⚡ **ARROW ATTACK** In 2011, New Zealander Matthew Scheurich survived being shot with arrows in a remote jungle area of Papua New Guinea by a tribesman who wanted him dead so that he could marry his French girlfriend. Scheurich sustained an arrow wound to the stomach, which luckily stopped just short of his aorta (the body's most vital artery), and another to his right lung, and was pelted with rocks. He was airlifted to a small hospit where X-rays showed that his chest was half-filled with blood. He underwent an emergency transfusion to prevent him from bleeding to death.

Peeing into a bucket!

# Urine Eggs

In Dongyang County, China, buckets of boys' urine are collected from local schools—for use in a culinary dish! Cooking eggs in urine to make Tong Zi Dan (small boy eggs) is believed to ward off ailments and promote energy. The eggs are soaked in boiled urine for an entire day before they are ready to eat, and remain popular with locals, despite advice from doctors in the area who say that Tong Zi Dan is potentially toxic.

**SNAKE BLOOD** After falling down a 79-ft-deep (24-m) pit in Changshan County, China, while hunting snakes, Yi Guofang survived for two days by killing one of the snakes he had captured, drinking its blood, and eating the flesh raw.

**UNUSUAL DRINK** A $250-million water-recycling device aboard the International Space Station enables astronauts to drink their own urine.

**LARGE FRIES** Five staff from the Fish and Chip Shop at the Adventure Island fun park in Southend, England, cooked up the world's biggest portion of fries in June 2011, weighing in at 988 lb (448 kg). It took about four hours to peel, cut, and fry the potatoes, which were then served in a box measuring 54 x 46 x 30 in (137 x 116 x 75 cm).

**PIZZA PASSION** There are more than 61,000 pizzerias in the United States and Americans eat about 100 acres (40 ha) of pizza every day, or 350 slices per second.

**EVERYTHING MUST GO** Yukako Ichikawa, a chef in Sydney, Australia, gives a 30-percent discount to all customers at her restaurant who eat everything on their plate—excluding only lemon slices, ginger, and wasabi.

**EDIBLE TABLE** Using 14 propane grills and 110 tables, volunteers at Crazy Otto's Empire Diner in Herkimer, New York State, cooked a 2,128-sq-ft (197-sq-m) omelet from 41,040 eggs. Using green food coloring, they turned it into an edible pool table with beach-ball billiards and broomstick cues.

**EXPLODING MELONS** Thousands of watermelons exploded in China's Jiangsu Province in the spring of 2011 after farmers sprayed their crops too freely with chemicals designed to make the melons grow faster.

**COSTLY SMASH** A forklift accident smashed hundreds of bottles of Australian wine worth a total of $1 million. All but one of the 462 cases of Mollydooker Wines' Velvet Glove Shiraz bound for the United States was destroyed. Each bottle sells for around $200.

**HOT DOG BET** Jim Harrison, a 22-year-old student at McMaster University, Hamilton, Canada, won a $1,500 bet by eating 450 hot dogs in a month—an average of 15 a day.

**PIZZA PICKUP** David Schuler of Jackson, Mississippi, makes a round trip of more than 2,800 mi (4,500 km)—just for pizza. Unable to find a pizza to his taste in Mississippi, he drives through 16 states to the Town Spa Pizza in Stoughton, Massachusetts. On one trip he bought 150 pizzas at a cost of $1,200.

# SPORTING CELEBRITIES

Singer **BILLY JOEL** was a welterweight boxing champion in his youth.

Actor **HUGH LAURIE** rowed for the defeated Cambridge crew in the 1980 Oxford–Cambridge University Boat Race.

In 1955, singer **JOHNNY MATHIS** was ranked tied for 85th in the world for the high jump.

Actor **RYAN O'NEAL** boxed as a teenager in Golden Gloves contests, finishing with a record of 18–4, including 13 knockouts.

Actress **GEENA DAVIS** narrowly missed out on being selected for the U.S. archery team to compete at the 2000 Olympics.

Writer **EDGAR ALLAN POE** once held the University of Virginia long jump record of 21 ft 6 in (6.5 m).

Iron Maiden frontman **BRUCE DICKINSON** was once ranked seventh in the U.K. for the foil discipline of fencing.

Actor **CHUCK CONNORS** played professional baseball for the Chicago Cubs and Brooklyn Dodgers, and basketball for the Boston Celtics.

**SIR ARTHUR CONAN DOYLE**, creator of Sherlock Holmes, played soccer for Portsmouth and cricket for the M.C.C., once bowling out the great W.G. Grace.

# FREAK INJURIES

- Toronto Blue Jays baseball player **GLENALLEN HILL** badly cut himself after falling out of bed and crashing into a glass table while having a nightmare about being covered in spiders.

- British cyclist **MARK CAVENDISH** was snowboarding on a Nintendo Wii video game when he fell off the board and injured his calf.

- Chicago Cubs baseball player **SAMMY SOSA** strained a ligament in his back as a result of a violent sneeze.

- Scottish golfer **SAM TORRANCE** cracked his sternum after colliding with a large plant pot in his hotel room while he was sleepwalking.

# 6 EXTREME RACES

The YUKON ARCTIC ULTRA is a grueling 430-mi (692-km) marathon on mountain bike, skis, and foot where temperatures can drop to –58°F (–50°C) plus windchill, making it the coldest race on the planet.

Crossing mountain routes through Germany, Austria, Switzerland, and Italy for eight days, the 200-mi (320-km) TRANSALPINE RUN has a vertical ascent of over 49,200 ft (15,000 m).

The six-day MARATHON OF THE SANDS covers 150 mi (240 km) of Moroccan desert, one-fifth of which is run over strength-sapping sand dunes in 122°F (50°C) heat.

Competitors in the NORTH POLE MARATHON run on ice for 26.2 miles (42 km) around the North Pole in temperatures of –22°F (–30°C).

The BADWATER ULTRAMARATHON is run over 135 mi (217 km) in California's Death Valley, starting at 282 ft (86 m) below sea level and ending at an altitude of 8,360 ft (2,548 m). Temperatures top a blistering 120°F (49°C) in the shade.

Brazil's seven-day JUNGLE MARATHON is run over a distance of 150 mi (240 km) through the treacherous Amazon rain forest. Competitors sleep in hammocks along the route.

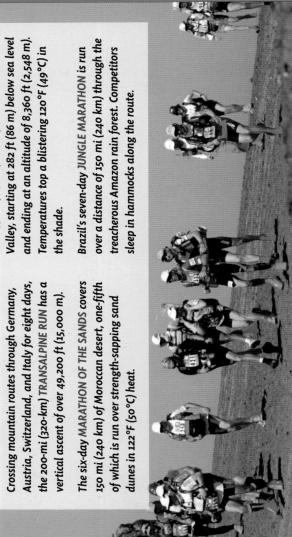

## Totally Bizarre

- Detroit Tigers baseball player **BRANDON INGE** strained a muscle while placing a pillow behind his son's head.

- Former Manchester United goalkeeper **ALEX STEPNEY** dislocated his jaw after yelling at his teammates during a match.

- Competing in Rome, Italy, long jumper **SALIM SDIRI** was speared in the side by a wayward javelin thrown by Finland's Tero Pitkamaki who had slipped at the end of his run-up. The javelin penetrated 4 in (10 cm) into Salim's flesh.

- Detroit Tigers' pitcher **JOEL ZUMAYA** missed three games after straining his arm playing Guitar Hero on a PS2.

- U.S. boxer **DANIEL CARUSO** broke his own nose while psyching himself up for a fight by pounding his gloves into his face.

- Celebrating a goal he had helped to set up for Swiss club Servette, soccer player **PAULO DIOGO** lost a finger after his new wedding ring caught in the wire fence surrounding the field. To add insult to injury, the referee yellow-carded him for excessive celebration.

- Boston Red Sox baseball player **WADE BOGGS** hurt his back when he lost his balance while trying to put on cowboy boots.

- New Zealand cricketer **TREVOR FRANKLIN** was ruled out of action for 18 months after being run over by a motorized luggage cart at an airport.

- San Diego Padres baseball player **ADAM EATON** accidentally stabbed himself in the stomach with a knife while trying to open some DVD packaging.

- In an infamous WBA Heavyweight Championship fight on June 28, 1997, **MIKE TYSON** bit off a chunk of Evander Holyfield's right ear and spat it on the ring floor.

# WEIRD SPORTS EVENTS

- Held annually in Finland, the Wife-Carrying World Championships are raced over an obstacle course, the winner receiving his wife's weight in beer.

- For the Great Klondike Outhouse Race, teams steer decorated outdoor toilets around the streets of Dawson City, Canada. One person has to sit on the toilet throughout the 1.5-mi (2.4-km) run.

- At Australia's Sheep Counting Championships, hundreds of sheep run across a field as competitors count them.

- The World Gravy Wrestling Championships take place annually in Lancashire, England.

- At the Emma Crawford Coffin Races, colorful coffins containing a living person are wheeled by teams along a course in Manitou Springs, Colorado.

- Sydney, Australia, stages a race solely for women wearing stiletto-heeled shoes.

- In the World Bog Snorkeling Championship, competitors wear snorkels and flippers to race in a Welsh peat bog.

- The International Cherry Pit Spitting Championship at Eau Claire, Michigan, sees competitors spit their pits distances of more than 90 ft (27.4 m).

# 9 SUPERSTITIONS

beverage called Pripps—and only if it had exactly two ice cubes in the cup and was delivered by the same trainer.

Baseball player **WADE BOGGS** always ate chicken before each game, took batting practice at 5.17, did running sprints at 7.17, and drew the word *Chai* (Hebrew for "Life") in the dirt before coming up to bat.

U.S. golfer **JACK NICKLAUS** always carried three pennies in his pocket for luck.

Basketball star **MICHAEL JORDAN** wore his lucky University of North Carolina shorts under his Chicago Bulls uniform in every game. To cover them, he started wearing longer shorts, which inspired an NBA trend.

Former New York Mets baseball star **TURK WENDELL** used to brush his teeth between innings, chew black licorice, and draw three crosses in the dirt then wave at the center fielder before he pitched.

Whenever he won a tournament match, Croatian tennis champion **GORAN IVANISEVIC** would repeat everything from the previous day—such as going to the same restaurant, eating the same food, and talking to the same people.

The night before every game, basketball player **JASON TERRY** goes to bed wearing the shorts of the next day's opposing team. He also plays in five pairs of socks.

South African golfer **GARY PLAYER** would only play with even-numbered balls; he left the odd-numbered ones in his bag.

Tennis player **SERENA WILLIAMS** always bounces the ball five times before her first serve and twice before her second serve.

Between hockey periods, one-time Philadelphia Flyers goaltender **PELLE LINDBERGH** would drink only a Swedish

# Scary Ride

An ultra-light plane hangs 33 ft (10 m) above ground from a Ferris wheel after crashing into it at a fair near Taree, Australia. The pilot and his passenger were trapped in the plane for nearly three hours, but they eventually walked away unhurt while two children who were trapped on the ride at the time also escaped injury.

**NO PANTS** On January 9, 2011, an estimated 3,500 commuters stripped down to their underwear and boarded subway trains across New York City for the tenth annual No Pants Subway Ride. The event has spread across the globe with tens of thousands of people taking part in 50 cities from Adelaide to Zurich. A modest band of 100 people rode the London Underground; and in Johannesburg, South Africa, 34 no-pants riders were arrested for public indecency before being released without charge.

**SHARK ATTACK** Kaiju Sushi and Rice Balls, a restaurant in New Smyrna Beach—the Florida town dubbed the shark attack capital of the world—offers a free shark sushi roll for anyone who has survived being bitten by a shark... and can prove it. The first customer to take advantage of the deal not only had a scar on his leg but also a YouTube video of himself on the local news in 2008 being taken away to the hospital.

**TREE BED** A woman fell fast asleep curled up on the narrow branch of a tree 20 ft (6 m) above the streets of Lanzhou, China. Shoppers realized she was there only when one of her shoes fell off and hit someone on the head.

**MOVING EXPERIENCE** Since getting married in Yorkshire, England, in 1955, Orina Wyness has lived in 60 different houses. She had to move every time her husband Ray, a naval petty officer, was given a new posting. Their globe-trotting took them all over the U.K. as well as to France and Australia, sometimes living in a house for just a few weeks.

**HIDDEN LOBSTERS** A shopper from Biloxi, Mississippi, was arrested for having two live lobsters in his shorts. The man was accused of trying to walk out of a grocery store without paying for food items that he had stuffed down his cargo shorts, including two bags of jumbo shrimp, a pork loin, and the lobsters. Police said he had tried to escape by throwing the pork at store employees.

**BAGELHEADS** The latest body modification craze in Japan is the "bagelhead," created by injecting a saline solution into the forehead so that it inflates alarmingly. Body inflators feel only a dull headache during the procedure, and their forehead takes about two hours to swell up. Many then prod their lumps to create more interesting shapes, after which the inflation goes down overnight, usually leaving no scars.

**NOT SO OLD** In July 2010, Japanese officials went to congratulate Sogen Kato on his 111th birthday for being the oldest man in Tokyo but instead found his mummified remains lying in bed—where he had died three decades earlier.

**HOLE SWEET HOME** For more than 20 years, Miguel Restrepo has lived with his wife Maria in a converted abandoned sewer pipe in Medellin, Colombia. The pipe, which is also home to their pet dog Blackie, is just 10 ft (3 m) wide, 6.6 ft (2 m) deep and 4.5 ft (1.4 m) high, but it has been fitted with a fan, a stove, a bed and even a TV. At night he covers the entrance with planks.

**BOY STOWAWAY** A nine-year-old boy flew alone from Minneapolis, Minnesota, to Las Vegas, Nevada, without a ticket or boarding pass. He went through security checkpoints at Minneapolis–St. Paul International Airport without being detected, but once he was on board the plane the flight crew became suspicious and arranged for him to be met by Las Vegas police on landing.

## BATMAN COLLECTOR

Chloe Konieczki from Belvidere, Illinois, is a Batman fanatic! She collects anything she can, from shirts to toothbrushes, and has even called her cat Batman. Her bedroom is black and yellow and she wants to be Batman when she grows up!

## EXPENSIVE CRASH

The Chugoku Expressway in Shimonoseki, Japan, was the scene of one of the most expensive and exclusive car wrecks in recent years. A total of 14 sports cars, including eight Ferraris, a Lamborghini, and a Mercedes worth something in the region of $1.3 million, were caught out on a drive to a supercar meeting in Hiroshima. It is thought the Ferrari owners may have been driving too close to one another when one driver lost control, leaving them little time to react before smashing into each other and careening into the road barrier.

**SCREAMING CORPSE** A 50-year-old South African man who was thought to be dead suddenly woke up after spending 21 hours in a morgue refrigerator. When the man screamed to be let out of the morgue in Libode, Eastern Cape, two mortuary attendants ran for their lives, believing he was a ghost.

**HUMAN PARCEL** Reluctant to pay the train fare, the parents of four-year-old May Pierstorff mailed her instead by U.S. Mail to her grandparents' home in Lewiston, Idaho. As her 48½-lb (22-kg) weight was just below the 50-lb (22.7-kg) limit, on February 19, 1914, they attached 53 cents in parcel post stamps to May's coat and she traveled the entire journey in the train's mail compartment before being delivered to her grandparents' home by the mail clerk.

**VAMPIRE CONFERENCE** Three hundred exorcists from all over the world traveled to Poland's Roman Catholic Jasna Góra Monastery in 2011 for a week-long congress to discuss the increase of vampirism in Europe.

**ORNAMENTAL SKULL** A dead man's relatives sued Czech police after officers used his skull as an ornament. The skull—wearing a police cap—was used as a bookend by officers at Volary who also took pictures of it and posted them on the Internet.

Distal
phalanges

Metacarpal

Proximal
phalanges

# BONE JEWELRY

Columbine Phoenix from Somerville, Massachusetts, makes jewelry from human bones. Among her creations are an earring with a middle finger bone, a necklace from five fingertip bones, and a necklace from a hand bone. She obtains the bones from universities and medical schools, and always uses hand bones because they are the only ones small enough for jewelry.

# UPSIDE DOWN

Mr. Zhu rode a bicycle upside down for a quarter of a mile (400 m) in Shaoxing, China. His feet were tied tightly by two belts connected to the bike, and his head rested on the saddle.

◪ UNUSUAL MOTIVE Jobless Richard Verone, 59, raided a bank in Gastonia, North Carolina, and demanded just $1—because he wanted to go to prison in order to receive medical treatment. After the robbery, he calmly waited inside the bank for police officers to arrive and arrest him.

## ◤ A QUARTER OF YOUR BODY'S BONES ARE IN YOUR FEET. ◢

◪ DEADLY REVENGE A fighting cock took deadly revenge on its owner for forcing it back into the ring too soon. Birds are usually given an hour's rest before fighting another opponent, but when Singrai Soren of West Bengal, India, repeatedly tried to push the cockerel back into the ring, it attacked him and slit his throat with the metal blades attached to its legs.

◪ STUCK IN CHIMNEY The remains of Joseph Schexnider, who went missing in 1984, were found 27 years later wedged in the chimney of the Abbeville National Bank in Abbeville, Louisiana. Schexnider, who died of dehydration after getting stuck in the chimney, may have been trying to break into the bank at the time. He had been hiding from police after skipping a court hearing over charges of possessing a stolen vehicle.

◪ SUICIDE WATCH Don Ritchie of Sydney, Australia, lives across the street from the Gap—a rocky cliff along Sydney Harbor. So far, he has saved more than 160 people from committing suicide by convincing them not to jump from the cliff.

◪ MISTAKEN ASHES Burglars who raided a home in Silver Springs Shores, Florida, thought they had stolen a quantity of cocaine, only later to realize they had actually discovered the cremated remains of a man and two dogs.

# Index

## ACKNOWLEDGMENTS

**Front cover** (t) Craig Sullivan, (b) Mooshikq - the World's smallest e-bike - Made in India by Santhosh, Mysore http://santhoshbikes.blogspot.in/; 4 Joshua Carter; **6–7** Nippon News; **8** (t) New Zealand Herald; **9** Courtesy of Ugly Models; **10** (b) Keisuke Yamada/Rex Features, (t) Anthonioo; **11** Benjamin Brown; **12** Phillips de Pury & Company; **13** (l) James R. Ford, (r) © Polaris/eyevine; **14** Nippon News; **15** (t) Crown Copyright: Department of Conservation Te Papa Atawhai (11 December 2011), Photographer: Christopher Clark, (b) USA National Parks Service; **16** Ze Frank/Rex Features; **17** (t) Mooshikq - the World's smallest e-bike - Made in India by Santhosh, Mysore http://santhoshbikes.blogspot.in/, (b) Feature China/Barcroft Media; **18** Reuters/Navesh Chitrakar; **19** Swns.com; **20** (t) Craig Sullivan, (b) John Luther Garcia; **21** Dimitri Tsykalov/Landov/Press Association Images; **22–23** Circus World Museum, Baraboo, Wisconsin; **24** (l, c) Sipa Press/Rex Features, (r) Joshua Carter; **25** Geoffrey Robinson/Rex Features; **26** (t) Chris Antes, (b) PizzaExpress/Rex Features; **27** Quirky China News/Rex Features; **28** (t) Sipa Press/Rex Features, (b) Reuters/Rafael Marchante; **29** (t) Jed Jacobsohn/Getty Images, (b) Reuters/Toby Melville; **30** (t) AAP Image/Press Association Images; **31** Chloe Konieczki; **32** Toshiro Kubo/AP/Press Association Images; **33** (t/l) Columbine Phoenix, (t/r) © Dario Sabljak/Fotolia.com, (b) Wenn.com; **Back cover** Chris Antes

Key: t = top, b = bottom, c = center, l = left, r = right, sp = single page, dp = double page

All other photos are from Ripley Entertainment Inc.
Every attempt has been made to acknowledge correctly and contact copyright holders and we apologize in advance
for any unintentional errors or omissions, which will be corrected in future editions.